CHRIS SLOANE

Small Business Internet Marketing Guide

How To Triple Your Sales And Turn Your Small Business Website Into An Online Lead Generation Machine

First published by Heaviside Group LLC 2020

First edition

ISBN: 978-1-7353136-0-3

This book was professionally typeset on Reedsy.
Find out more at reedsy.com

Contents

1

INTRODUCTION

Thanks for reading our Small Business Internet Marketing Guide!

In this guide we will walk you through the important things you need to do to establish an effective online presence and explain:

- How the search engines work and what you need to do to handle each part of them for maximum visibility and return.
- How the map listings work and how to get your small business company listed on the map.
- Our search engine optimization strategy for small businesses.
- Our social media strategy specifically for small businesses.
- Our paid search strategy designed to be effective for small businesses.

I am excited to be sharing this information with you. There are tons of information sources out there from lots of so-called experts, but it can be very hard to tell what is good information and what is not.

What we show you in this book is based on working with over 1,000 customers across the entire world. We like to keep track of where we have helped people – this map is current as of June 2020:

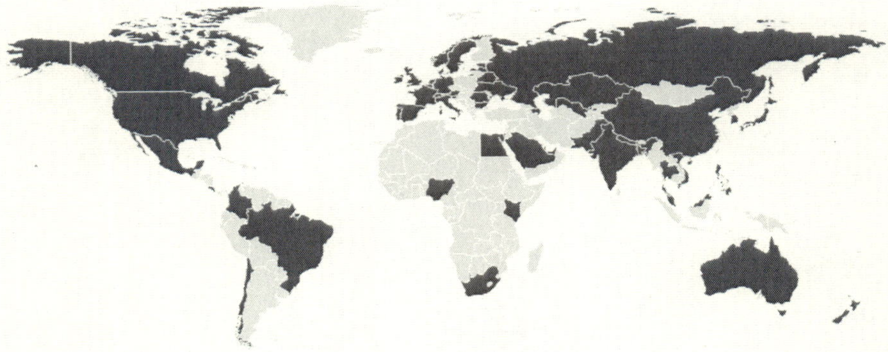

We have customers on all six inhabited continents, so we have seen a lot and have learned a lot about what works well and what might not.

What we find is while the inputs might be different – keywords change, offers are different, business economics and acceptable cost per leads vary – the fundamentals ring true for everyone.

Those fundamentals are what we are going to cover in this guide.

Who Am I?

Before getting too deep here I would like to introduce myself. Who am I and why should you listen to me?

My name is Chris Sloane. I am the founder of Heaviside Group. I have been working in SEO, web development, and digital marketing for over 10 years.

My background prior to that was in physics – and while it may seem unrelated, the process of breaking something down to find out why and how it works is very relevant to this profession. Unlike physics, the rules are constantly changing as the search engine algorithms evolve. What worked well a year ago is often not quite the same today.

I have worked with international enterprises to SaaS companies to small retail storefronts. While I cannot say we have seen it all, I can say we have seen enough!

Everything I will be talking about here has been learned "in the trenches" on real projects that helped grow leads and sales for businesses of all types.

What We Do

Spoiler alert: our company does this stuff. My team has built websites, attracted search engine traffic, driven profitable paid visitors, increased conversion rates with retargeting, and on and on.

We have a proven process designed to triple your sales by getting your internet marketing right. That process is what this book is based on.

We would love the opportunity to work with you and do this for your business. But that is not what this book is – it is not going to be a hidden sales presentation that is going to require you to buy services from us to *really* make things work.

I want to give you the best information out there on how to do this stuff for your own business. If you take this information and implement the process, it is going to work for you, and you are going to succeed.

Thanks again for checking out our book!

Chris Sloane

Founder, Heaviside Group

2

WHY SEO IS SO IMPORTANT FOR SMALL BUSINESSES

Most business owners already understand that the internet & search engines are *extremely* important to the long-term growth and sustainability of their business. But occasionally I am asked something like this:

"Why are search engines and search engine marketing so important to small businesses?"

There are several good answers here – and it does need to be addressed. A huge number of SMBs (small-to-medium businesses) do not invest enough in their online marketing efforts and are hurting their business growth in the process.

Yellow Pages Are No Longer Effective

It used to be that the number one place consumers looked when they needed a small business service was the Yellow Pages. In today's market, very few people still reference the printed Yellow Pages. In fact, the newer generations have not even been exposed to the Yellow Pages and only know the internet to search for local businesses.

Where do they go now?

They look on the search engines (Google, Yahoo, Bing & others) and social media sites (Facebook & Twitter) asking for referrals from their friends and family.

- A recent survey of 2,000 consumers found that 86 percent of those surveyed used the internet to find a local business.
- 74 percent of the respondents said they use a search engine when they are looking for a local retail or service business.

If you are not showing up on page one of Google, Yahoo & Bing for the small business-related keywords in your area, then you are missing a major opportunity.

In this guide we will show you how you can ensure that you put your best foot forward and show up in as many local small business-related searches in your area as possible.

3

UNDERSTANDING HOW SEARCH ENGINES WORK

Over the past ten years the way the search engines work has changed significantly - especially with the introduction of the Google Map listings to the search results for local search.

Most of the small business owners we talk with are confused about how the search engines work and the differences between the map listings, organic listings and the paid (pay-per-click) listings.

In this section we wanted to take a few minutes to explain the search engines and break down the anatomy of the search engine results page (SERPs). By understanding how each component works, you can formulate a strategy to maximize the results of each.

There are 3 core components of the search engines results page:

1. Paid / PPC Listings
2. Map Listings
3. Organic Listings

Let's take a look at them one by one.

Pay Per Click Listings

In the paid section of the search engines you are able to select the keywords that are relevant to you and then pay to be listed in this area.

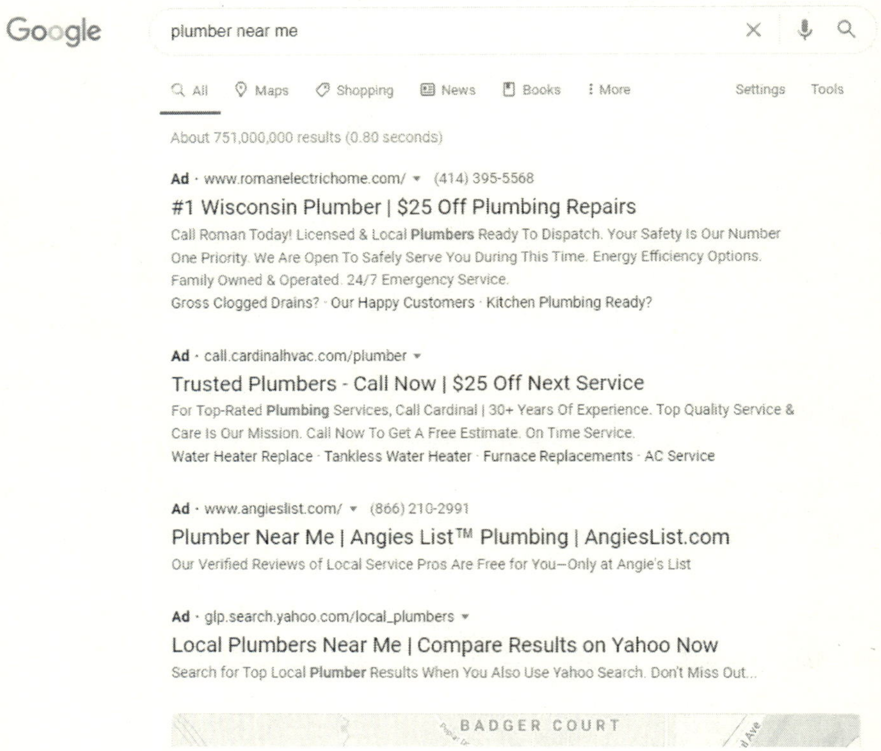

These are almost always at the top of the search results for "commercial-intent" keywords – i.e. the keywords searchers use when they want to buy something.

The reason these are called "Pay-Per-Click" or PPC is because rather than paying a flat monthly or daily fee for placement, you simply pay each time someone clicks on the link.

The cost per click is based on a bidding system. The company that bids the highest *with the best quality match between the ad, search, and landing page* gets the best placement. Great ads and landing pages can reduce your costs significantly – we have seen reductions of over 50%!

PPC is still a great way to market your business online, but it has to be approached carefully. PPC can get very expensive very fast, with some keywords costing as much as $60.00 per click or more in some industries.

Map Listings

The map listings have become very important because it is the first thing that comes up in the search results for most locally based searches after the ads. If someone searches "[your main keyword] + your city" chances are the map listings will be the first thing they look at.

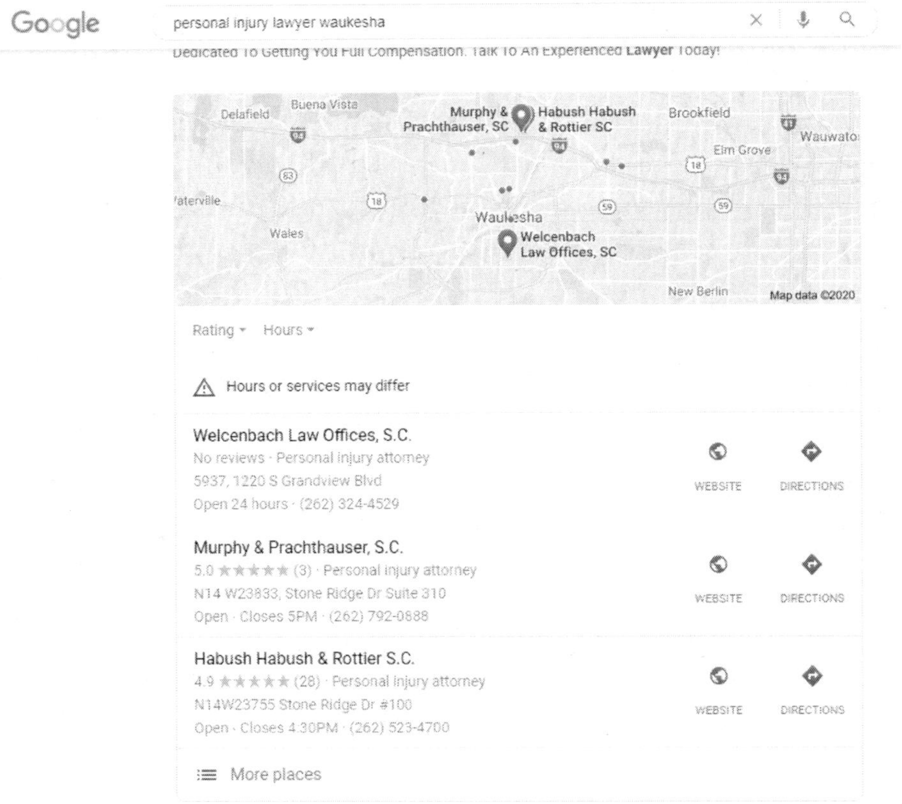

Unlike the paid section of the search engine, you can't buy your way into the map listings you have to earn it, and once you do, there is no per click cost associated with being in this section of the search engine.

Note that Google will sometimes show ads in the map listing, but typically on the "More Places" section. They experiment with placements quite a bit, and it changes from time to time as they do.

We will share our Google Maps optimization strategy with you later in this guide and show you exactly what needs to be done to obtain page one placement in the map section of the search results.

Organic Listings

The organic / natural section of the search engine results page appears directly beneath the map listings in many local searches, but appears directly beneath the paid listings in the absence of the map listings.

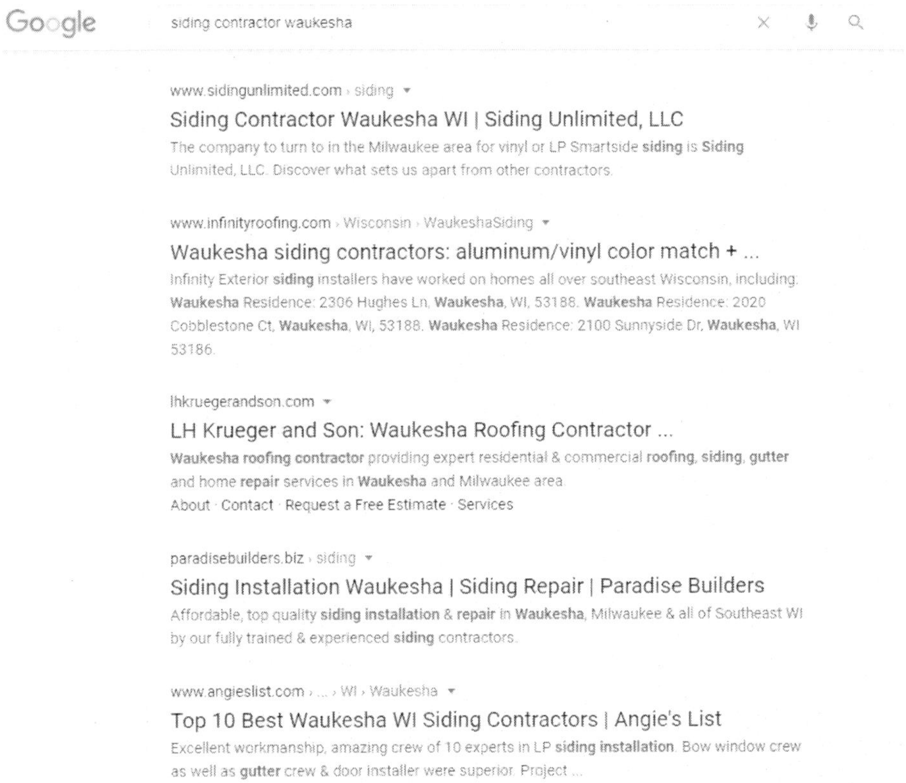

Similar to the map listings, you can't pay your way into this section of the search engines and there is no per click cost associated with it. We will share our search engine optimization strategy with you later in this guide.

Now that you understand the 3 major components of the search engine results and the differences between paid listings, map listings & organic listings you might wonder… "What section is most important?"

This is a question that we receive from business owners every day.

The answer is **all of them**.

All three components are important, and each should have a place in your online marketing program because you want to show up as often as possible when someone is searching for your services in your area. With that said, assuming you are operating on a limited budget and need to make each marketing dollar count; you need to focus your investment on the sections that are going to drive the strongest return on investment.

Research indicates that a vast majority of the population look directly at the organic & map listings when searching and their eyes simply glance over the paid listings.

However, many leads do come in through the paid listings – so active buyers tend not to ignore them.

If you are operating on a limited budget and need to get the best bang for your buck, you should start by focusing your efforts on the area that gets the most clicks at the lowest cost. We have found that placement in the organic and map section on the search engines can drive a *significantly* better return on investment than PPC marketing.

So how can you get your small business company listed in the organic and map listings?

That is what we are going to be covering in the following chapters.

4

GETTING YOUR BUSINESS ON GOOGLE MAPS

For a local business, the best return-on-investment (ROI) lead generator is without question the Google Map listings. We are going to cover how to show up on the maps.

The Google Map result is what shows up when someone types in "your city" plus "your services" in Google.

Set Up Your Google My Business Listing

The most important thing you have to do is go to https://www.google.com/business/ and claim your "Google My Business" listing.

Before you do that, go ahead and check if your listing is already set up and just not claimed. Go to Google Maps (maps.google.com) and search for your business.

If your business has been around for a while, you are probably already in there. If it has not been claimed yet, you will see something like this:

Go ahead and click "Claim this business" to start the process.

Some things to be aware of as you claim your Google My Business listing. The process is relatively simple. If you have a Gmail account or some type of Google account, Google should recognize that and let you use that to claim your listing. If you do not, you are going to need to go through the process of establishing a Google account so that you can claim your Google My Business listing.

The most critical part of the setup process is to verify your business. They will typically mail a card to your business address with a code you need to enter into your GMB back end. Do not skip this step, because it will hurt your abilities to show up and rank well.

The actual setup is very straightforward - it is going to walk you step by step through the process. You are going to type in your company name, address, and phone number. Make sure all of that information is correct.

Use your actual company name. If your business is "Roof Tech Incorporated," make sure that you enter, "Roof Tech Incorporated," and not something else like "Roof Tech Roofing Services" or "Roof Tech, Your Dallas Roofing Company." Do not add additional keywords in that name. It is against the Google My Business rules and policies and your listing could be deleted.

It is important that your Name, Address, and Phone Number (referred to as your "NAP") is correct. This is part of your online "fingerprint" and it will be critical that it is consistent as you take other steps in the ranking process.

If your address includes a Suite number, use it the same way each time. Either "Suite 300" or "#300" but not both in different places. Be consistent. If you are not sure which one to use, use the version Google shows when you search for your business.

Fill out all of the information fully and completely. Do not skip anything. If you do not have photos, go take them – both inside and outside of the office. Get a shot of your whole team together if you can.

Record a video introducing your business. It does not have to be "professionally done." Your customers are going to connect with real content – they are going to get a sense of who you are and what you are about. You only have 30 seconds to work with, so no need to overthink it.

List your hours, phone number, services, etc.

The most important section of all is your **categories**. This is how Google knows where to place your business in search results for Maps.

These are our categories.

We are going to show you now how to pick them.

First, write down a list of your biggest competitors in your area. Pick the top 5 or 6 of them, especially those that you think have been doing a decent job online or have worked with SEO companies.

Now, go to Google Maps again and search for them – and write down the category you see.

Their category is "HVAC contractor"

Their category is "Heating contractor"

Their category is "Air conditioning contractor"

You might see 3-5 different terms in the categories, or you might see only one that shows up consistently. That is OK.

Now, search for those **categories** in Google Maps and see what shows up.

You should start seeing patterns. One category should show up more often than others when you see your competitors. *Choose that one as your primary category.*

Then, add all of the other ones you saw as you were researching this as long as they are relevant to your business. You will end up with something like this:

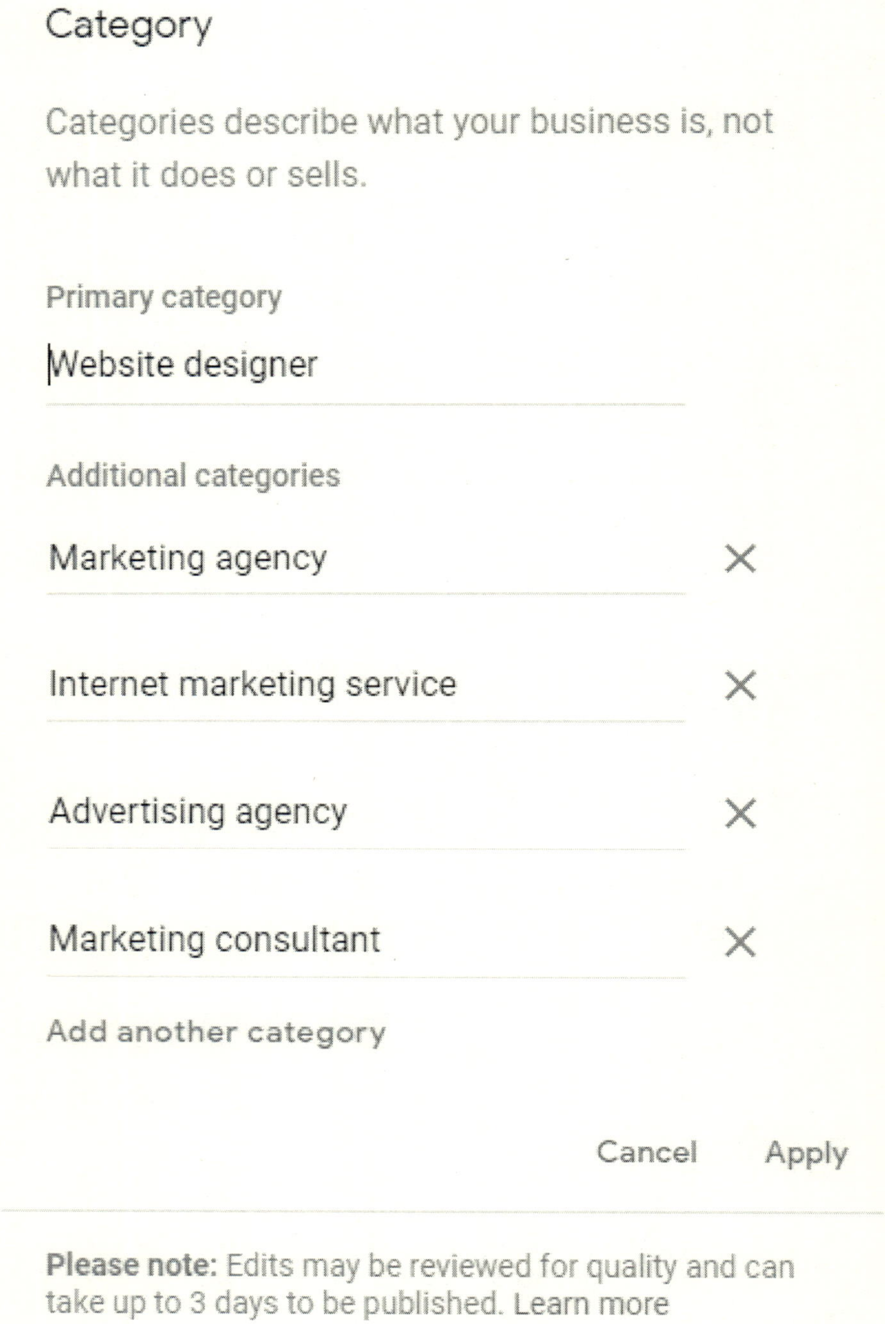
Category
Categories describe what your business is, not what it does or sells.
Primary category
Website designer
Additional categories
Marketing agency
Internet marketing service
Advertising agency
Marketing consultant
Add another category
Cancel
Apply
Please note: Edits may be reviewed for quality and can take up to 3 days to be published. Learn more

That is it, your GMB listing should be set up correctly.

Once you are verified, come back and test it from your office location. Type in your categories in Google Maps and see if you show up. If you know the keywords your customers would use to search for you, try those too. If you do not know them, we will cover that later.

Getting your listing in place is just the start of what you need to do. You are going to need to build a special kind of backlinks to support your listing, called *citations.*

I will use one of our nearby competitors to illustrate how important this is – keeping identities private of course.

When you just set up your Google Maps listing and leave it at that, you can expect to show up in a pattern that looks like this:

Each number is a spot on the grid where the maps ranking was measured – and is the location where the company showed up in the listings. Only spots 1, 2, and 3 are visible without clicking through to "more places" and those top spots get the vast majority of clicks.

You can see our competitor shows up for "Waukesha seo company" in the small area around their office but is essentially invisible to the rest of the city.

This is what you can expect to see when you first set up your GMB listing – but if you do the work of link building, you can expect to see something like this:

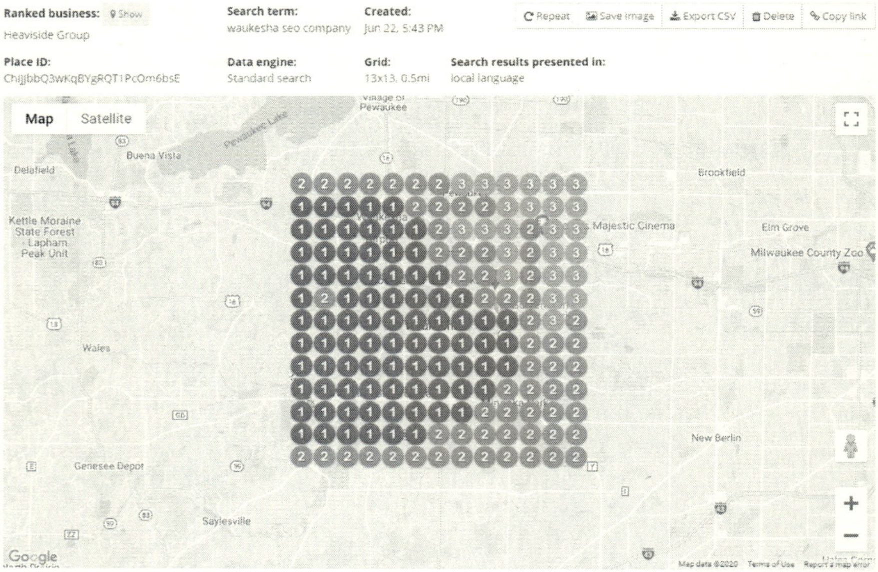

We are visible to everyone in the entire city. It also persists if someone does not use the "your city" + "your service" version:

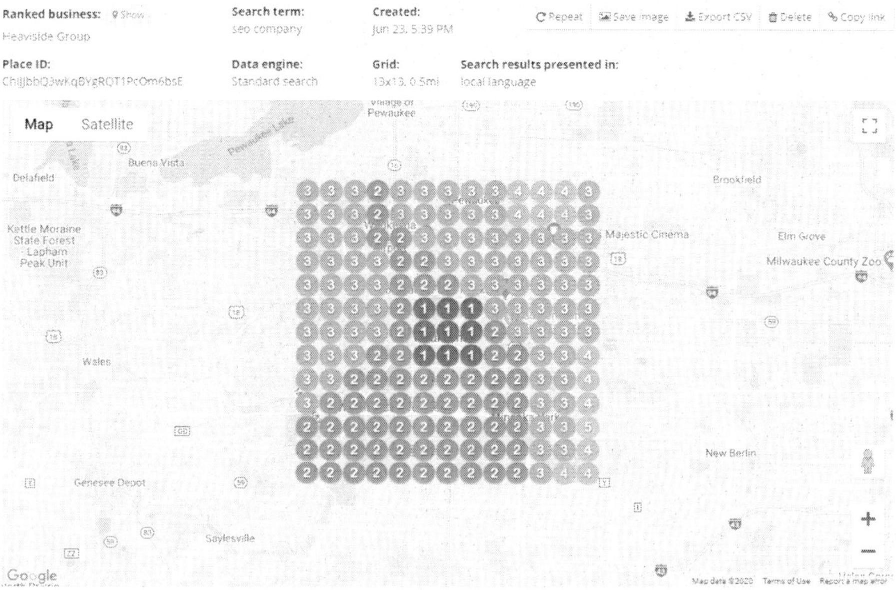

Keep in mind that Google gives a **strong** advantage to "close" businesses when someone is searching for a term. Most searches are mobile now, and when someone uses their phone Google knows exactly where they are and tends to show the closest businesses to them that match their query.

But – if your business sends **strong signals** that it is the authoritative or best one in the area, Google will show you over some nearer locations that might not be as strong.

There are more than 20 marketing companies in that area covered by the grid, or at least over 20 that actually show up in maps. *We are showing up in the top 3 map pack across the entire city.*

That is your goal with Google Maps. Part of that is driven by how you structure your site, but as I mentioned above building citations is a huge part of it.

Building Citations

If there is a site I *really* do not like, it is Yelp.

We have had the unfortunate situation of dealing with fake reviews – and one malcontent in particular went above and beyond, leaving the same fake review on every site he could find.

He was not even a customer of ours – we refused to work with him because his company dealt with adult-themed topics and drugs, and we did not want to participate in that. He took offense and left fake reviews everywhere.

It was a major pain, but I got them removed everywhere – except one place: you guessed it, Yelp.

This is the company that buried several actual reviews from customers and left up the one fake one – and refused to take it down after multiple complaints and calls. .

I have talked to others who have had the same issue with them – they are a pain to deal with and I don't use them for anything.

Except for one thing – a citation.

I tell this story because many local business owners can relate to Yelp problems – but also everyone knows who they are. It is a perfect example of a citation link.

Remember NAP? Name – Address – Phone. This is the core of citation building. Find as many sites as you can that will let you make a listing on there and do it. You are going to want dozens, if not hundreds of them.

Now – who has time for that? Not me. Fortunately, there are solutions for you to consider making the process easier.

We use BrightLocal – it locates relevant citations for our business and will go out and build them for us for a small fee.

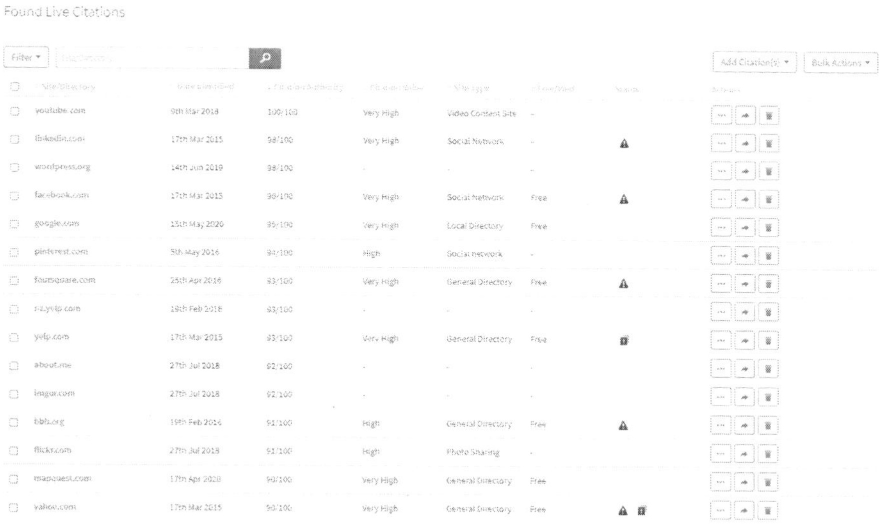
Found Live Citations

Filter | Add Citation(s) | Bulk Actions

youtube.com	9th Mar 2018	100/100	Very High	Video Content Site	-
linkedin.com	17th Mar 2015	98/100	Very High	Social Network	-
wordpress.org	14th Jun 2019	98/100	-	-	-
facebook.com	17th Mar 2015	96/100	Very High	Social Network	Free
google.com	15th May 2020	95/100	Very High	Local Directory	Free
pinterest.com	5th May 2016	94/100	High	Social network	-
foursquare.com	25th Apr 2016	93/100	Very High	General Directory	Free
nz.yelp.com	19th Feb 2016	93/100	-	-	-
yelp.com	17th Mar 2015	93/100	Very High	General Directory	Free
about.me	27th Jul 2018	92/100	-	-	-
imgur.com	27th Jul 2018	92/100	-	-	-
bbb.org	19th Feb 2016	91/100	High	General Directory	Free
flickr.com	27th Jul 2018	91/100	High	Photo Sharing	-
mapquest.com	17th Apr 2020	90/100	Very High	General Directory	Free
yahoo.com	17th Mar 2015	90/100	Very High	General Directory	Free

There are other options you can look at too. Moz Local offers a service, as does Yext.

They all do essentially the same thing – get your citations in order. The key thing here: your NAP must match your GMB listing and must match your website.

Pick one and get it done, that is it.

One more point to make here – you also want to build non-citation links to enhance the authority and strength of your domain. That has a very strong impact on the **organic** listing, but also influences your ability to show up in wider area on maps.

This is a pretty broad and complex topic to try to tackle here – there are lots of ways to go about doing this. We like to look at what links our competitors have and try to go get them – especially if those competitors are outranking us. There are lots of tools out there that can help you find out what links your competitors have – we use Ahrefs.

Here are a few examples – you might find that your competitors have a link from the local chamber of commerce. Are you a member of the chamber and have a link back to your site from them? If not, join. It is a good thing to do anyway.

You might see they have links from local newspapers. How did they get them? Can you get written up in an article on their website? Was it from a press release that was picked up?

They might have links from non-profit organizations in the area. Are they serving on the board? Did they make a contribution or gift, or volunteer their time?

Find out how your top competitors are getting links and do likewise.

Next, we are going to look at a factor that might surprise you.

Reviews

That negative review attack from that disgruntled "customer" was a real pain to deal with. It took a lot of time to resolve and it is still out there thanks to a certain terrible review site.

What do reviews have to do with ranking in the maps? Plenty!

There is no study that I am aware of that definitely shows ratings are a maps ranking factor – but there are certainly "secondary" metrics that indicate that they must be.

For example – one known ranking factor is the "click-through-rate" or CTR. This is what percent of the time searchers click on your result for that keyword. The better your CTR is relative to your ranking position, the more of a ranking boost you get. This is because Google's business model hinges on searchers getting the result they are looking for. If searchers tend to click on your site, that tells the algorithms that your site is clearly relevant to the search query.

Lots of positive ratings are a huge CTR-driver. Think about how you shop online. Are you clicking on the result that has only a few or poor reviews? Of course not – you are going to click on the one that has the most positive reviews.

We notice that the top-reviewed companies in an area tend to have a stronger maps presence. Whether that is from CTR or from reviews being included in the ranking algorithm is unclear, and it does not matter. Either way, you need to consistently get as many good reviews as you can.

There are a bunch of good options here too – we use BrightLocal for this as well. BirdEye is an option, as is NearbyNow. There are others too. Just pick one that makes sense to you and you will use and get it integrated into your customer service process.

Do not neglect this – it is one of the most important things you can do to take care of your online reputation.

Remember that goofball that gave us a bad review? We got rid of that one, but we have another fake one on Google we cannot shake. One-star, was never a customer, we have no idea who did it.

Can you tell?

No, you cannot, because we have 37 other 5-star reviews that bury it.

Most of your potential customers are not going to dig into the details right away – they will make snap judgments based on the overall rating. Anything below 4 and you are in trouble. They might investigate, but more than likely they are just going to click on your competitor who took reviews seriously.

The more reviews you have, the merrier. We have several marketing channels in place and have had a few difficult customers. We do not worry about those customers anymore, because no single unfair review can shake our online reputation – the quality of our work is very, very clear.

If you take action on anything in this guide – take action on this. Bad reviews are the silent online leads killer.

Google My Business Optimization Best Practices

There are several best practices that you want to be aware of to properly optimize your Map listing.

- *Company Name* – Always use your legal Company Name – do not stuff additional fields into the Name Field i.e. if your company name is "Joe's Roofing" don't try to stuff additional keywords like "Joe's Roofing – Dallas Roofers". This would be against the Google My Business guidelines and will reduce your probability of ranking. It might work for a bit – but then you will get caught and slapped down. We have tested it – do not bother!

- *Address* – On the "Address Field" use your EXACT legal address. Be intentional here. You want to ensure that you have the same address listed on your Google My Business listing as it is on all the other online directory listings like YellowPages.com, CitySearch.com, Yelp.com, etc. The consistency of your NAP (Name, Address, Phone Number) is very important for placement.

- *Phone Number* – Use a local (not 800#) and use your real office number rather than a tracking number. We find that 800#'s don't rank well. If you use a tracking number it will not be consistent with your other citations and ultimately won't rank well.

- *Categories* – You can use up to five categories, so use ALL five. Be sure to use categories that Google is telling you that your competitors are using and that reflect actual business you do. If you are a plumber and that is all you do, do not list HVAC categories just because you saw one of your competitors using it.

- *Service Area & Location* – Make sure you set this up accurately. If you do not serve an area, do not say you do. If you have multiple locations, set separate service areas for each one and make sure they do not overlap. Also, if you do not have a location in an area do not try to fake one with a UPS Mailbox or something like that. Google is wise to that one and it tends not to work.

- *Picture and Video* – Use this opportunity to upload authentic content about your company. Do not use stock photos, it is obvious and looks really bad. Just be authentic and give people an idea about who you are. Most people do not even look at this.

- *Reviews* – As we mentioned above, just make sure you have a process in place for this. Print out "Review Us" cards with instructions on how to do.

Keep an eye out for very happy customers that might be willing to leave one for you. Send an email to your established client base with a link for them to click. There are lots of ways to do it!

5

ORGANIC SEO STRATEGY FOR SMALL BUSINESSES

SEO, or Search Engine Optimization, is the process of getting your website to show up in the organic (free / non-PPC) section of the search engines.

There are specific things that you can do both on and off your website to ensure that you show up when someone types "your service" + "your city" into Google, Yahoo or Bing. In all of our years working with small business clients in some of the most competitive markets in the United States, we have developed a proven strategy that consistently gets our clients to the top of the search engines and we are sharing it with you in this section.

Build Out Your Website To Capture More Search Terms

Search engines rank *pages*, not websites. Each page on your website can really only be successfully optimized for **one** main keyword.

A typical small business site has only 5-6 pages (Home – About Us – Our Services – Coupons – Contact Us). That does not create a lot of opportunities to rank for different terms. Now, most pages will rank for more than one term – but they will be closely related. If you offer several different services, you are not going to rank for all of them with one page.

Many small businesses provide a wide variety of services. A roofing company, for example, will do roof installation and roof repair, and might even do siding or windows. By *building* out the website and creating separate pages for each of these services (combined with city modifiers), the small business contractor can get listed on the search engines for each of those different keyword combinations. Here is an example:

• Home – About – Coupons – Contact Us

• Sub Pages for Each Service – Miami Roof Installation, Miami Roof Repair, Miami Siding Installation, etc

They often provide services in a large number of cities outside their primary city. In order to be found on the major search engines for EACH of those sub-cities, additional pages need to be created:

• Sub-pages for each sub-city serviced – Kendall Roof Installation, Doral Roof Installation, Homestead Roof Installation etc.

A quick note here about duplicate content. You cannot use exactly the same content for Miami Roof Installation and Kendall Roof Installation or those pages will get penalized – Google's algorithms don't like that. So the content on those pages has to be *unique*. Focus the page content more on the sub-area you are targeting and keep it simple. You do not need a long novel here; these sub-area keywords tend to be relatively less competitive and easier to rank for. Start with 500-750 words and see how it does for you.

Optimize Pages for Search Engines

Once the pages are built for each of your core services and sub-pages, each of the pages need to be optimized from an SEO perspective so that the search engines understand what the page is about and list you for those words.

This is a very active area of development in SEO, and there is a huge move towards analyzing search engine results with statistical methods to see what ranking factors are the most important for each search term. We spend a lot of time doing this for our customers and it is become a key component of our on-page SEO strategy. That approach is very advanced and is outside of the scope of what most business owners will want to take on. Fortunately, there are some basics that are straightforward that can go a long way towards getting you ranked for the search terms that matter for your business.

If your website is built using WordPress, install the Yoast SEO plugin. There are others (we are partial to Rank Math) but Yoast is the most well known and is easy to use. This plugin will allow you to take care of most of these tasks without having to get into the website code.

Here are some of the most important items that need to be taken care of for on-page search engine optimization:

Unique Title Tag on each page – each page should have a unique title tag that no other page on your site has. It should include the keyword you want to rank that page for. We recommend this format: "Keyword Phrase You Want to Rank For | Your Brand" – for example, "Miami Roofing Contractor | Joe's Roofing"

H1 Header Tag on each page – this should be the keyword phrase you want to rank for. So, from our example above we would use "Miami Roofing Contractor." Key point: do **not** use more than one H1 per page. Think of your web pages like an outline, and the H1 is the topic of our outline. The other header tags (H2, H3, and so on) are the bullet points beneath that topic. Would your outline make sense if it had more than one topic? No, and your page will not either. The H1 is the strongest signal in the body text area and you do not want to dilute it.

Other than that, just follow the guidelines that Yoast gives to optimize that page. They are not perfect, but it is going to get you close enough to be reasonably competitive. These will be things like adding keywords to the paragraph text and meta descriptions.

Make sure to create and set up the XML sitemap as well. Yoast will create one for you, and you will want to take that link and update Google Search Console with it. This is important because it lets Google know what pages you have on your website instead of relying on Google to find them. They are pretty good at doing that but giving them a sitemap ensures that all of your sub-pages will be found and likely indexed.

Inbound Links

Once your pages are built and the on-page optimization is complete, the next step is getting inbound links. The more competitive your niche and area are, the more of them you will likely need.

You have already built a solid link baseline with your citations, and we mentioned some competitor link-building possibilities previously. If you are not seeing enough traction with what you have done already you will have to get more aggressive in building links. They are still one of the strongest ranking signals that Google uses to assess website quality.

There are basically two approaches you can take here: do this yourself or hire a link-building service to do it for you.

We recommend the second approach. If you can allocate a budget of at least

$300-$500 per month for links you can build some solid authority over time and enhance your competitiveness tremendously.

If you do not have a budget to do that, I would suggest continuing with the competitor backlink strategy. Those links can be challenging to get, and at some point you are going to run out of them, but they can be enough to do the job.

If you do have the budget, there are many different link providers out there. We have used https://authority.builders/ and https://nobs.link/ before.

That's it for SEO – while each section has a ton more stuff you can do, and we do more for our clients, doing these things will put you ahead of many of your competitors and take you a long way towards winning the organic search results.

6

SOCIAL MEDIA STRATEGY FOR SMALL BUSINESS

There is a lot of interest around social media (Facebook, Twitter, etc), but how can it be leveraged by small business owners? How can you actually use social media to grow your small business?

It depends a lot on what niche you are in. Some businesses tend to be more active on social media than others, but there are some commonalities that you should take advantage of.

There are two main things to understand here. First, social media is a huge source of "word of mouth." If you think about it, where do most conversations happen now? Sure, you still see people in person and chat with them – but far and away most social interaction occurs on these platforms. Potential customers are going to check out your business on there. They might ask their friends for recommendations. They will read your recommendations. In a lot of ways managing this is like managing your reviews.

Another aspect to consider here is recency – if your last social media post was 2 years ago people may wonder if you are still doing business. It might seem silly, but for heavy social media consumers activity on the site can signify activity in the "real world." You want to keep your social media profiles up to date and active for the same reason you update your website footer every year – it tells people you are still active. (You do that, right? If your footer says copyright 2016, put down this book and go change that right now!)

The second main thing to understand about social media is that it has become a huge source of entertainment.

The latest statistics indicate that the average social media user spends **2 hours and 23 minutes per day** browsing their feeds.

Compare this to the numbers from the Q1 2019 Nielsen Total Audience Report about hours spent watching TV per day. People aged 50+ spend about 6.5 hours per day. Those aged 35-49 spent roughly 3.75 hours per day. The 18-34 age group *spent just under 2 hours per day.*

People under 35 spend more time on social media than they do watching TV.

This trend is not likely to reverse – and so your business needs a strategy to be visible there.

Unfortunately, Facebook wised up to this years ago and the chances of your social media posts getting much widespread traction are slim-to-none. The Facebook news feed is pay-to-play, and so you must consider running Facebook Ads.

This is a huge topic and is too broad to cover here, but we can go over some basic principles that will be helpful.

First – we do **not** recommend that you try to run Facebook Ads yourself unless you take the time to learn how to do so. The interface is complicated and confusing, and there are many pitfalls that can lead you to set them up incorrectly. You also need the Facebook Pixel installed on your website or you cannot take advantage of the tracking and optimization features that are available. You also lose some of your best targeting options, like showing ads to people that are statistically similar to visitors to your website.

Second – you have to carefully consider *where* you are sending that traffic. Dumping Facebook Ads visitors onto your homepage is not going to do much for you.

Facebook Ads are interruption marketing – similar to TV commercials, except you can click on them and interact with them. That is the power of them, but also the danger. People are not looking for your product or service when they are on Facebook, they are looking for cat videos or updates from friends they have not talked to in years. If you catch their attention and they interact, you must make it easy for them to do what you want them to do, or they are going to go right back to cat videos.

Third – do not boost posts. It does not do anything useful for you.

Fourth – there is one type of campaign that every single business should do on Facebook, and if you are not, you are missing sales.

You need to set up retargeting campaigns based on visitors to your website, so that anyone who visits your website sees an ad from you on Facebook. Everyone knows about these ads (why is that vacuum cleaner following me around on the internet???) and some people are annoyed by them, but they have consistently been shown to improve conversion rates.

Why?

Because people shop, and they often do not make a decision right away. They may have checked out your website, and a few of your competitors, and ultimately decided "I'll do this later."

If you're showing them ads across the internet between the time they looked at your site and the time they decide to take action, and your competitors are not, who do you think is more likely to be remembered and have the best chance at the sale?

There's a lot more that can be done here, but if you have up-to-date social media channels, engage your customers with content, get their recommendations, and run ads to let them know about your business you are way ahead of most companies out there.

7

PPC STRATEGY FOR SMALL BUSINESS

This is another subject that is broad and tough to tackle here, but we can outline a general approach that will be appropriate for any small business.

The Two Main PPC Platforms

There are really two main players in the Pay Per Click space – Google, and Bing. Google has the vast majority of the market share, while Bing also serves ads on Yahoo and AOL Search (yes, it still exists!).

We recommend ignoring Bing as you get started. You are going to want to test things in Google, get them working right, and show that you can run ads profitably there. Then, you can simply import what is working into Bing. They are no fools, and they make it very easy for you to do that.

Some people will include Facebook in the PPC category and it is true, that is one of the payment models they have. The more common way to categorize these channels is "Search Engine Marketing" (SEM) and "Social Media Marketing" (SMM) and SEM is typically the one people have in mind when they say PPC.

We are going to focus now on Google Ads and restrict our discussion to them, as they are the most common ads and the ones you are going to want to do.

Types Of Google Ads

There are several different types of ads you can run on Google's networks.

Search ads – these are the ones that you probably think of when you think of "Google Ads." They are based on keyword searches and are associated with a Cost Per Click (CPC).

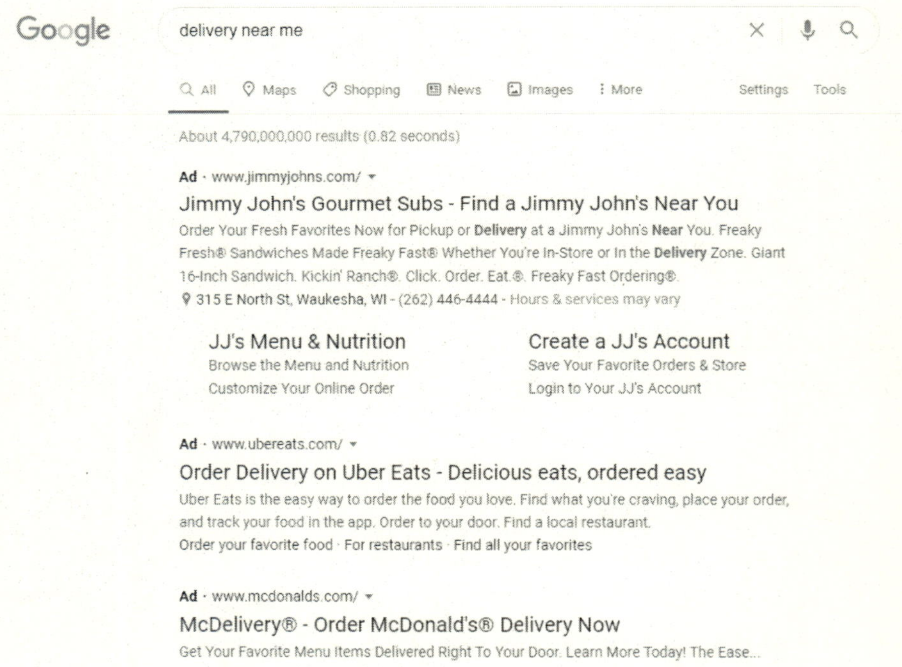

Display ads – these are the ads you see when browsing websites. There are really two main campaign types here.

Display network campaigns targeting people who visit specific websites or have different interests.

Retargeting campaigns that serve ads to people who visited your website.

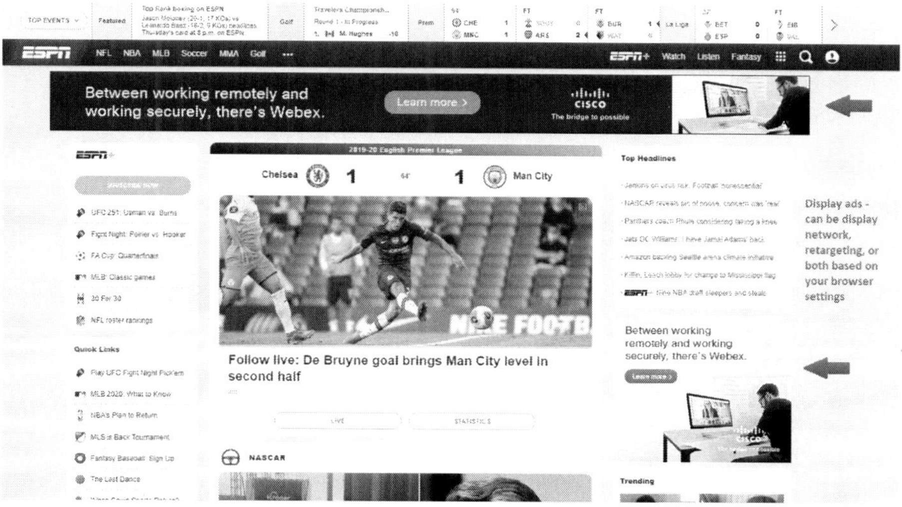

There is another, newer type of display ad called "discovery ads" that Google just rolled out to try to compete with Facebook's display reach. We will not cover those here.

Video ads – these are video-based ads that primarily run on YouTube. These are a bit more advanced and typically will not be a good fit for most small businesses, and so we will not cover them here.

There are a few other ad types – like Shopping ads – which are a bit advanced and not a good fit for most small businesses and we will skip those.

What Campaigns Small Businesses Should Run

There are two types of Google Ads campaigns we would advise all small business owners to consider running: search ads and retargeting ads.

For the search ads, there are a few things to keep in mind.

You should have a high-converting landing page to send the traffic to. Do not send paid traffic to your home page. You should consider implementing call tracking (check out Call Rail) on those landing pages to help measure the kinds of leads the ads are bringing in.

Do not advertise outside of your service area. You can avoid this by geofencing the area you want to show ads during the campaign setup.

You should have Google Analytics set up on your website, and should also have conversion tracking in place so that you can measure the results and what your return on investment is.

If you are going to advertise multiple services, you are going to need a different landing page for each one. The reason for this is Quality Score. This is how Google scores ad bid and rewards those it thinks will serve the best experience to clickers. That score depends on how well your ad text and landing page match up to the keyword the searcher clicked to get there. If you have a high quality score, you will be rewarded with lower Cost Per Click.

The most important thing about search ads is this: know your numbers. You need to know what your acceptable cost per acquisition is – if you can afford to pay $100 for each new customer and be profitable, then you better be sure you are not paying $150!

For your retargeting campaign, you just have to get the images made and fire it up – it's relatively simple to set up and since you'll be showing ads to people who visited your website, there is not a lot of complicated setup here.

There are a lot of little steps to setting up these campaigns and there are a lot of guide out there that can show you how to do that, so we won't use the space here to do so. However, we do want to show you an easy way to find the right keywords to start advertising with.

Keyword Research

If you have not done so already go ahead and set up your Google Ads account. We recommend using the same Gmail address you used to set up your Google My Business account.

Once you have that set up and you are in there, go to the "Tools" area and navigate to the Keyword Planner. It should look something like this:

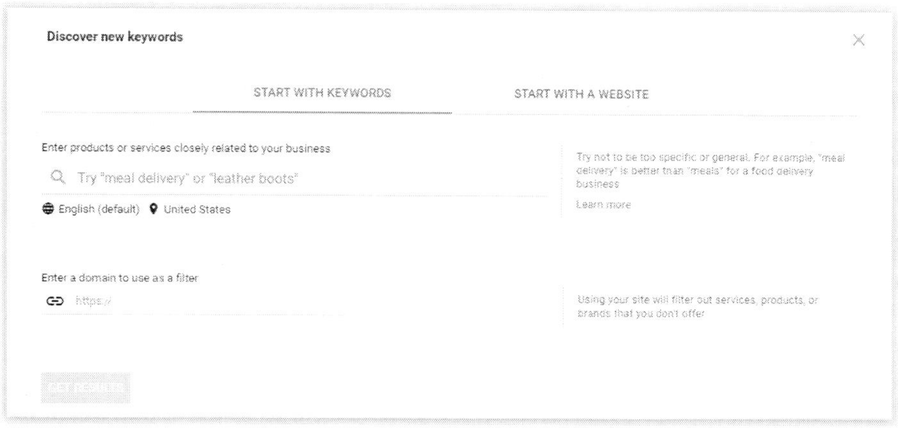

Remember the categories you picked when you set up your Google My Business? You are going to use that list here to find what keywords Google thinks is relevant to you. Start with your primary category – enter it in the search box there and click "Get Results."

In this example I am going to use "roofing contractors."

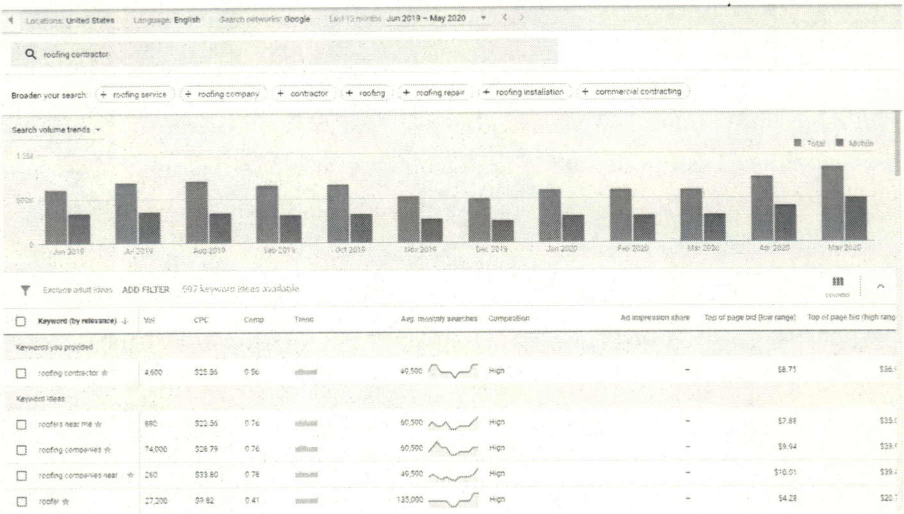

You can see that you get a ton of useful data here. Keep in mind that you are looking at data for the entire US, and that is ok. Remember that you are going to geofence your campaign to your service area.

Take a look at the "Top of page bid" estimates to get a sense of what you're going to need to be spending per click in order to be competitive. If you have everything set up well (high-converting landing page, great quality scores, etc) you can expect a conversion rate in the range of 5-10%. It can be higher or lower depending on the business type, but it is a good rule of thumb. Use those numbers as a sanity check on the bid prices here. Just because Google says that is what the bids should be does not mean you have to use them. You might find you can get away with bidding less in your geofenced area, and in fact you often can.

I would suggest downloading the keyword ideas and saving them.

The next thing you want to do is add your city modifier and see what happens:

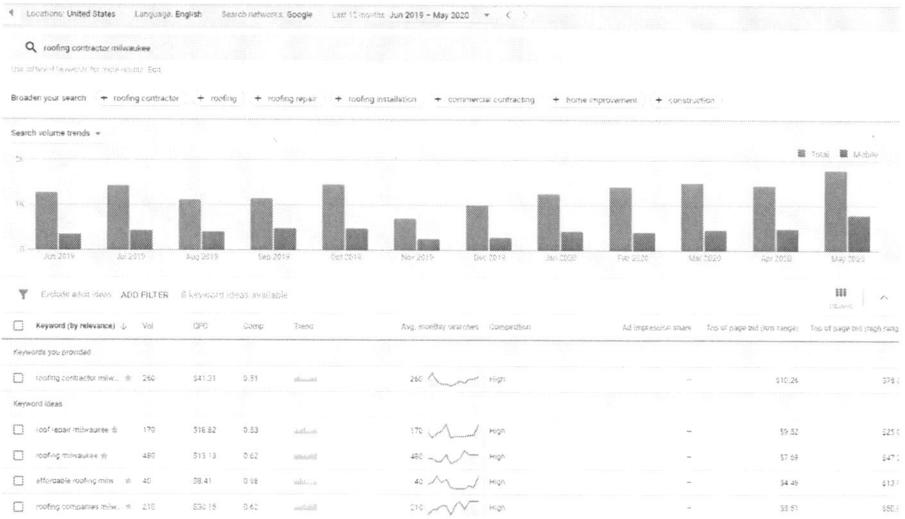

You are going to get a set of geo-modified keywords. Download those too. Repeat this for each major city in your service area that you do business in.

Now, repeat all of these steps for your other categories.

You are going to have a ton of useful information that will guide you in what to do next. At minimum, you are going to need a dedicated landing page for each service you want to run ads for. You can even make service + city landing pages if you want to get super-detailed and get the best possible quality scores.

Then, you are going to want to build search campaigns for each service type, with ad groups for each related sub-group of keywords. You can even do single-keyword-ad-groups (SKAGs) – which is the approach we prefer.

If you are new to Google Ads, or even trying it again – we suggest picking one key service and starting with that. Build your landing page, make sure all of the tracking is set up correctly, build and run the campaigns, and see if it's producing profitable leads for you. Once you have that first campaign working for you go ahead and import it into Bing.

Then, do the same thing for the next service you want to advertise.

It can be a lot of work, but it is a tried and true way to generate leads for small businesses!

8

FINAL THOUGHTS

If you have been implementing these things as you have gone through the book you should be in great shape now. You already should be seeing more leads and new customers from your efforts. Nice work!

If you are not there yet that is OK too. Pick the area you feel most comfortable tackling first and go from there. Depending on how much of this you have set up already (or have not set up) it might seem like a daunting task to wrap your arms around.

You may have read this book and concluded that you do not want to do any of this yourself. If that is the case, and you would like to consider working with us, here is what I would like you to do.

Go to https://www.heavisidegroup.com/book and schedule a call with me.

Here is what we are going to do for you:

Keyword Research – we are going to take a look at your business and put together a keyword list for you. We are also going to take a look at where you are ranking currently for those terms. This will help us figure out where you are at and what could use some improvement.

Conversion – we are going to take a look at your website and give you feedback on how it is set up. Will it work as is or does it need to be revised?

Authority – how are you doing with respect to your competitors? Are their sites much "stronger" than yours is? Can you compete effectively? How are you doing with reviews?

Plan of Action – we are going to recommend a course of action – what needs to be done based on where you are today to potentially double, triple, or 10x your sales over the next six to nine months.

Now, my time is valuable, and so is my team's. If someone asked us to put this report together for them, we would charge $349 for it. The value you can get from this information is far greater than that.

Frankly, at that price it is a steal.

However, you have made the commitment to invest time in reading my book and I appreciate that. Chances are if you are reading this part you have read the rest of it.

So, I am including a surprise bonus here – we will do this assessment for you for free as a thanks for doing that, subject to two commitments:

- If my team and I take the time to do this assessment for you, that you will show up for the call.
- If what we show you is compelling, you're serious about potentially hiring us to do this for you and take your internet marketing strategy and run it on your behalf, as we've done for hundreds of other clients.

If that sounds good to you, and you'd like to take us up on that, head over to https://www.heavisidegroup.com/book and schedule that call with me!

Made in United States
North Haven, CT
04 November 2026

21772123R00032